The Goose Girl

Activity Book and Play

Contents

Name: _______________________________

Class: _______   School: _______________

OXFORD
UNIVERSITY PRESS

Activities

Before you read, can you write the words?

> king   goose   hole   meadow   castle
> cupboard   ~~princess~~   gate   coin

1

princess

2

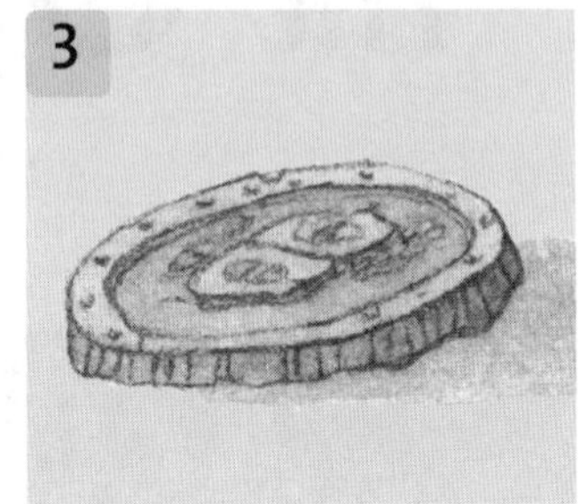

3

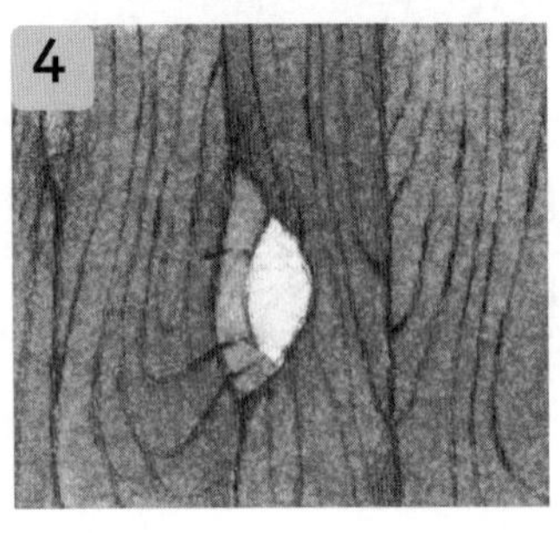

4

5

6

7

8

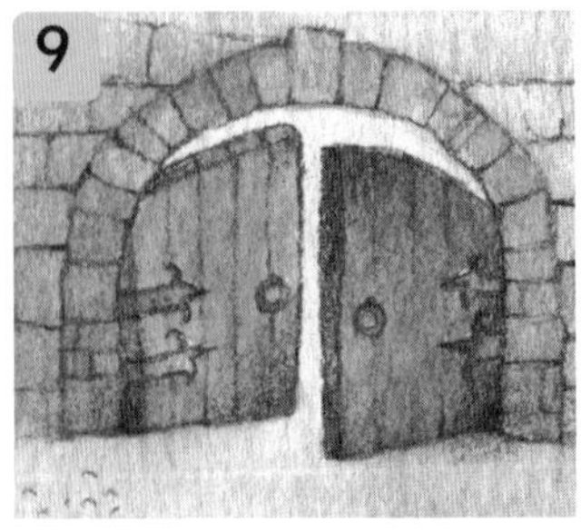

9

→ Pages 2–3

1 Write the words.

   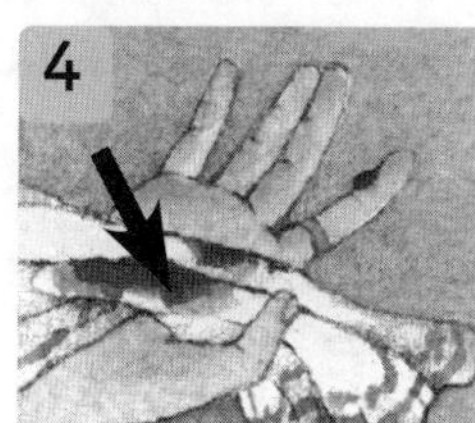

q e n u e	a i m d	h r o s e	l b o d o
queen	__________	__________	__________

2 Circle the correct words. Then complete the sentences.

1 The queen had a beautiful ____ _daughter_ ____.

   sister   friend   (daughter)

2 The day came for the princess to go ________________.

   far away   on a ship   to school

3 The princess was going to ______________ a prince.

   visit   look after   marry

4 The queen gave the princess a ________________.

   white flower   gold cup   black coat

5 And she gave the princess a ______________ horse.

   magic   bad   strange

6 The queen gave her daughter a maid to ______________
   with her.

   ride   jump   run

7 The queen made three ______________ fall onto a handkerchief.

   drops of milk   cups of water   drops of blood

8 The princess put the ______________ inside her dress.

   cup   handkerchief   money

Put the words in the correct order.

1 was It very a day hot.
   It was a very hot day.

2 thirsty Soon princess the was.

3 Please drink get of will me you a water?

4 horse it get your You off and get!

5 be I not will maid your!

6 not to princess know The what did say.

7 horse off So her got she.

8 the stream drank went to She and.

9 into handkerchief the fell The water.

10 dress me and off to that it give Take!

11 quick will Be or you now kill I!

12 to I going bride am the be.

13 And be are going to you maid my!

→ Pages 6–7

1 Write the words and number the sentences 1–5.

prince   gate   ~~maid~~   goose   castle

a ☐ The king said to the princess, 'You can be a ___________ girl.'
b ☐ The king and the ___________ came to meet them.
c [1] The ___*maid*___ rode in front of the princess.
d ☐ The king took her to a little house near the castle ___________.
e ☐ In the evening they arrived at the ___________.

2 Match, then write a sentence under each picture.

The real princess was left ...   to meet them.

The princess rode ...   to see Kirsten.

The king took her ...   outside.

The king and his son came ...   behind the maid.

1

The princess rode behind the maid.

2

3

4

→ Pages 8–9

1 Circle the correct words. Then write sentences.

1 That night, what was there at the castle?

(a big dinner)   a nice lunch   a lovely party

That night there was a big dinner at the castle.

2 Who told the prince to kill Falada?

the men   the king   the maid

____

3 What did the real princess give the men?

a gold coin   a handkerchief   a letter

____

4 Where did the men put Falada's head?

in a stream   by the castle gate   in a bag

____

2 Who is speaking? Write the name for 1–4. For number 5, what do the men say? Write one sentence.

1 'This princess is going to be my son's bride.'   *the king*

2 'That white horse, Falada, is a bad horse.'   ______________

3 'I will tell my men to take it away.'   ______________

4 'Put this horse's head by the big castle gate.'   ______________

5 ____   *the men*

→ Pages 10–11

1 Answer the questions.

1 Where are Kirsten and the real princess? _In the meadow._

2 Are there some geese in the meadow? _______

3 What is the real princess doing to her hair? _____________________

4 Who wants some of her hair? _____________________

5 Does the real princess want to give it to her? _______

2 Complete the sentences with the past tense of these verbs.

think   go   blow   answer   brush   walk   say   ~~take~~   speak   sing

1 Every day Kirsten _____took_____ the geese out to the meadow.

2 The real princess _____________ with her.

3 They _____________ through the castle gate.

4 Every day the real princess _____________ to Falada's head.

5 And the head _____________ her.

6 Kirsten _____________ it was very strange.

7 Every day the real princess _____________ her long gold hair.

8 Kirsten always _____________, 'Give me some of your hair!'

9 The real princess _____________, 'Blow, wind. Blow!'

10 Then a wind came and _____________ Kirsten's hat off.

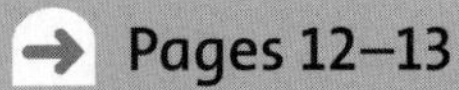

1 Write the words.

next   mad   ~~real~~   dead   true   angry

1 The ___real___ princess had time to brush her hair.
2 It made Kirsten _________ .
3 She went to the king and said, 'That girl is _________ .'
4 She told him, 'Every day she talks to a _________ horse's head.'
5 The _________ day the king hid and watched.
6 And he saw that it was _________ .

2 Put the words in the correct order.

1 run Kirsten the to over had all meadow.
   Kirsten had to run all over the meadow.

2 hair brush had Then princess real her the to time.

   ____

3 You're girl mad a.

   ____

4 the I'm tell to about going you king.

   ____

5 again her with want don't I work to.

   ____

6 to hat She off wind the blow asks my.

   ____

7 to and this I come see want.

   ____

8 So watched day hid the king next the and.

   ____

1 Choose a, b, or c.

1 Who spoke to Falada's head?

a ☐ the maid   b ☐ Kirsten   c ☑ the real princess

2 Who heard the princess sing to the wind?

a ☐ the king   b ☐ Falada   c ☐ the prince

3 Why did the real princess ask the wind to blow Kirsten's hat?

a ☐ So she had time to visit the prince.

b ☐ So she had time to brush her hair.

c ☐ So she had time to play with the geese.

4 Who spoke to the real princess that evening?

a ☐ Kirsten   b ☐ the maid   c ☐ the king

5 Why didn't the princess tell the king her story?

a ☐ Because she was tired.

b ☐ Because she was afraid.

c ☐ Because she was sad.

2 Circle the mistake in each sentence. Then write the correct word.

1 The king (let) the real princess speak to Falada's head. ___heard___

2 She said to Falada, 'Do you like me?' ___________

3 Falada said to her, 'You are the true maid.' ___________

4 In the meadow the king heard her sing to the sun. ___________

5 He saw Kirsten's hat fall off. ___________

6 He saw her run all over the garden. ___________

7 That morning the king spoke to the real princess. ___________

8 She said, 'I cannot tell you my game.' ___________

9 The king said, 'I will go out of the castle.' ___________

10 He said, 'You can tell your story to this old door.' ___________

Pages 16–17

1 Make sentences about the story. Then write them in the correct order.

The king found the prince ...

He told them about the real princess ...

The king listened through ...

Then the king told the princess ...

The princess got inside the cupboard and ...

told her story.

and they were happy.

a hole in the wall.

to come with him.

and all the people in the castle.

1 *The princess got inside the cupboard and told her story.*

2 ____

3 ____

4 ____

5 ____

2 What does the princess say? Write the words.

maid   help   true   kill   horse   ride   marry   ~~real~~

'I am the ___real___ princess – the _______ bride. My _______ is going to _______ the prince ... She took my _______, Falada ... She made me _______ behind her. I have no one to _______ me. She will _______ me if I tell anyone.'

→ Pages 18–19

Circle the correct words. Then complete the sentences.

1 That night the ___*true bride*___ sat next to the prince.

   kind king   (true bride)   real queen

2 Her maid sat on his other _______________.

   side   place   chair

3 After dinner, the king spoke to _______________.

   everybody   nobody   somebody

4 He said, 'I have _______________ to tell you.'

   an idea   something   a story

5 Then he said to the maid, 'Tell me what you _______________
   about this.'

   say   think   hear

6 The maid answered, 'Put that bad maid on a _______________.'

   goose   horse   ship

7 'And _______________ the mad, bad horse throw her into the sea!'

   watch   make   let

8 The king said, 'Right, then this is what
   _______________ to you!'

   will happen   I will do   I will say

9 So the maid had to _______________
   a mad, bad horse.

   find   ride   carry

10 And it _______________ her into the sea.

   threw   put   took

11 Then the prince _______________ the
   real princess – the true bride.

   talked to   looked for   married

Play

Act the play.

Characters

 Chorus

 Queen

 Princess

 Maid

 Falada (magic horse)

 King

 Prince

 Kirsten

 Men (2)

 People in the castle (4)
(no words to speak)

 Pages 2–3    **Scene 1**

Chorus: Once upon a time there was a queen. The day came for her daughter to go far away and marry a prince. The queen gave the princess a magic horse.

Princess: I love this horse, Mother. I will call it Falada!

Chorus: The queen made three drops of blood fall onto a handkerchief.

Queen: Take this. It will make you strong. Goodbye.

Princess: Goodbye, Mother! Thank you for everything!

 Scene 2

Chorus: It was a very hot day. Soon the princess was thirsty.

Princess: Maid! Please will you get me a drink of water?

Maid: No! You get off your horse and get it!

Chorus: The princess went to the stream and drank. Her handkerchief fell into the water.

Maid *(to herself)*: Now she has nothing to help her. *(to the princess)* Take off that dress and give it to me! Be quick now or I will kill you! I am going to be the princess.

Scene 3

Chorus: In the evening they arrived at the castle.

King *(to the maid)*: How do you do, Princess? This is my son, the prince! *(to the princess)* Who are you?

Princess: I came here as a maid, but you have many maids.

King: You can be a goose girl. Come with me.

Chorus: The king took her to a little house.

King: This is Kirsten's house. She looks after the geese.

Scene 4

Chorus: That night there was a big dinner at the castle.

King: This princess is going to be my son's bride.

Scene 5

Maid: That horse, Falada, is a bad horse. You must kill it!

Prince: Yes, my bride. I will tell my men to take it away.

 Scene 6

Chorus: The real princess heard about this. She ran to the men.

Princess: Take this gold coin. Do you see this dead horse? Put this horse's head by the big castle gate.

Men: What? That's a mad idea! Why?

Princess: Because I loved that horse. I want to see its face.

Chorus: The men put Falada's head by the castle gate.

Scene 7

Chorus: Every day Kirsten took the geese out to the meadow, and the real princess went with her. They walked through the castle gate.

Princess: Falada! My horse ... do you know me?

Falada: Yes, Princess! You are the true bride!

Chorus: Then the real princess brushed her long hair.

Kirsten: Give me some of your hair!

Princess: No, Kirsten! Stop it!

Chorus: But Kirsten wouldn't stop it.

Princess (*singing*): Blow, wind. Blow Kirsten's hat, so I have time to brush my hair!

Chorus: A wind came and blew Kirsten's hat off. Kirsten had to run all over the meadow. Then the real princess had time to brush her hair.

Kirsten: You're mad! I'm going to tell the king about you.

→ Pages 13–17

🍃 *Scene 8* 🍃

Kirsten: That girl is mad. She talks to a dead horse's head. And it talks back to her. And she sings to the wind.

King: Mmm! I want to come and see this.

🍃 *Scene 9* 🍃

Chorus: The next day the king hid and watched.

Princess: Falada! My horse! Do you know me?

Falada: Yes, Princess! You are the true bride.

🍃 *Scene 10* 🍃

Chorus: In the meadow the king heard the real princess sing to the wind.

Princess *(singing)*: Blow, wind. Blow Kirsten's hat, so I have time to brush my hair!

Chorus: The king saw Kirsten's hat blow off.

🍃 *Scene 11* 🍃

King: Who are you? What is your story?

Princess: Oh! She will kill me if I tell you anything.

King: You can tell your story to this old cupboard.

Chorus: The princess got inside the cupboard. The king listened through a hole in the wall.

Princess: I am the real princess. My maid took my dress. She took my horse. She will kill me if I tell anyone.

King: Do not be afraid! Come with me.

→ Pages 17–19

 **Scene 12**

Chorus: The king found the prince and all the people in the castle. He told them about the real princess. And they were happy. They could see that she was beautiful and good.

Scene 13

Chorus: That night the true bride sat next to the prince. Her maid sat on his other side and did not know her.

King: Listen! Once there was a princess who had a maid. She had to ride far away to marry a prince. On the way the maid said, 'Give me your dress! And give me your horse! Or I will kill you! I am going to be the princess now!' *(to the maid)* Tell me what you think about this.

Maid: Put that bad maid on a mad, bad horse. And let the mad, bad horse throw her into the sea!

King: Right, then this is what will happen to you!

Scene 14

Chorus: So the maid had to ride a mad, bad horse. And it threw her into the sea. Then the prince married the real princess – the true bride. And they were very happy.

 **The End**